This Notebook Belongs to

_____

A Apple

A A A A A A A

a a a a a a a

Aa Aa Aa Aa Aa

Ananas Ananas

B Bus

B B B B B B B

b b b b b b b

Bb Bb Bb Bb Bb

Better Better

C   Car

C c c c c c

c c c c c c c

Cc Cc Cc Cc Cc Cc

Cartoon Cartoon

D Dinosaur

D D D D D D

d d d d d d d

Dd Dd Dd Dd

Dolphin Dolphin

E Elephant

E E E E E

e e e e e e

Ee Ee Ee Ee Ee

Easter Easter

G Good

G G G G G G

g g g g g

Gg Gg Gg Gg

Green Green

H Hamburger

H H H H H H

h h h h h h

Hh Hh Hh Hh Hh

House House

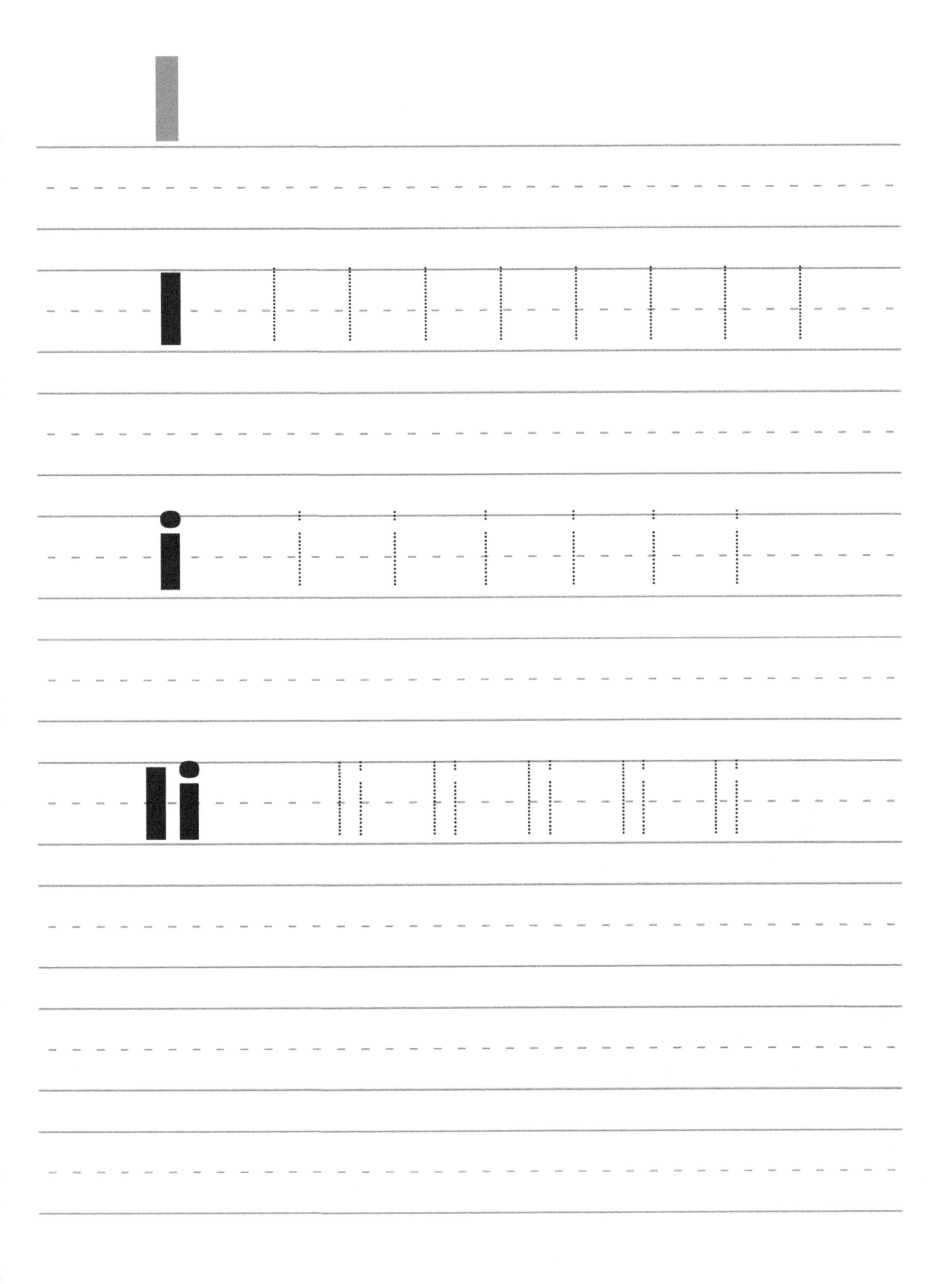

J Jack

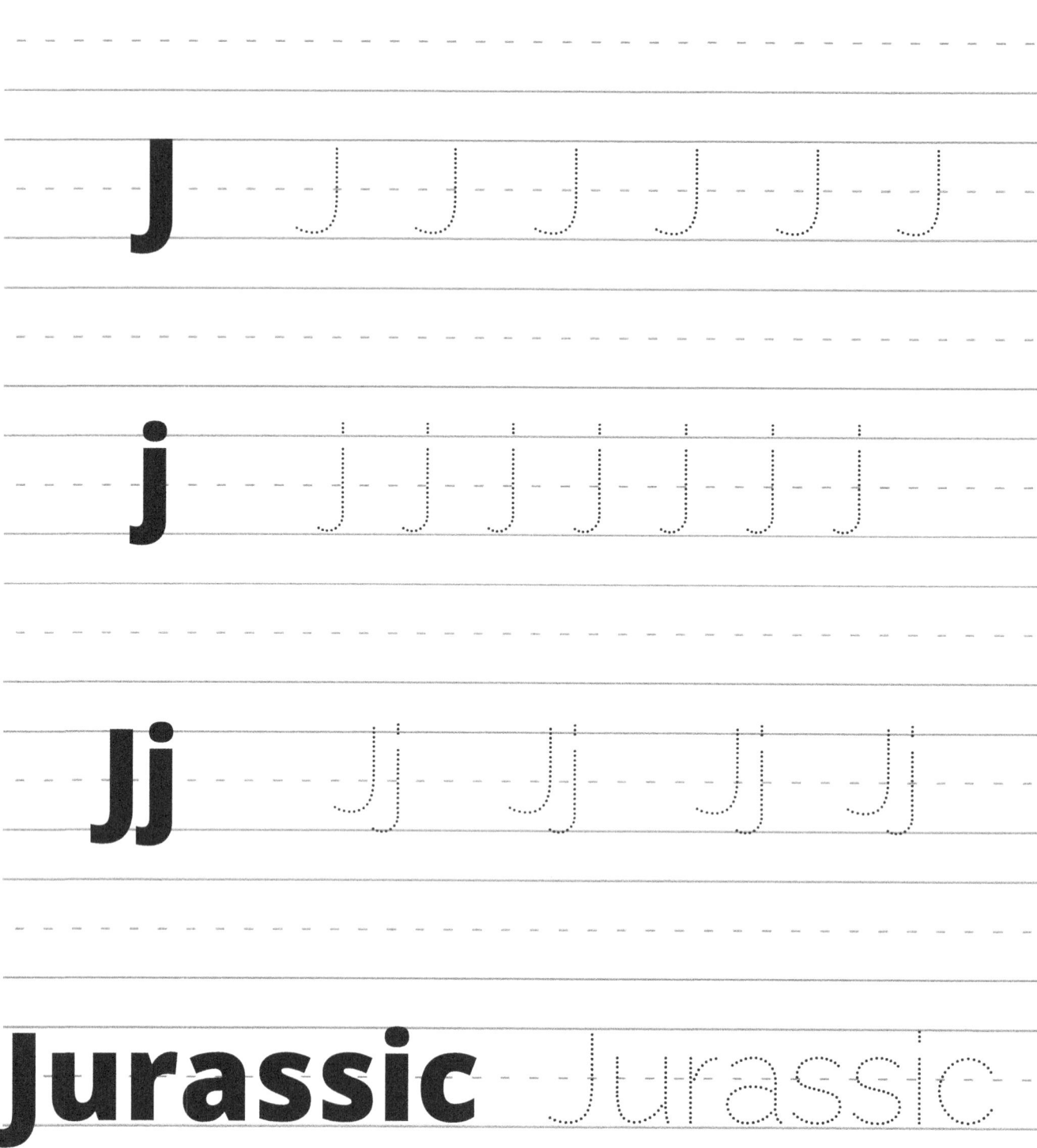

J JJJJJJ

j jjjjjjj

Jj Jj Jj Jj Jj

Jurassic Jurassic

K Kangaroo

K   Kk Kk Kk Kk

k   k k k k k

Kk   Kk Kk Kk

Kiwi   Kiwi

L Love

L L L L L L L

l l l l l l l

Ll Ll Ll Ll Ll

Lion Lion

M   Mom

M   M M M M

m   m m m m

Mm   Mm Mm

May   May

N Natural

N N N N N N N

n n n n n n

Nn Nn Nn Nn

Nail Nail

O   Opera

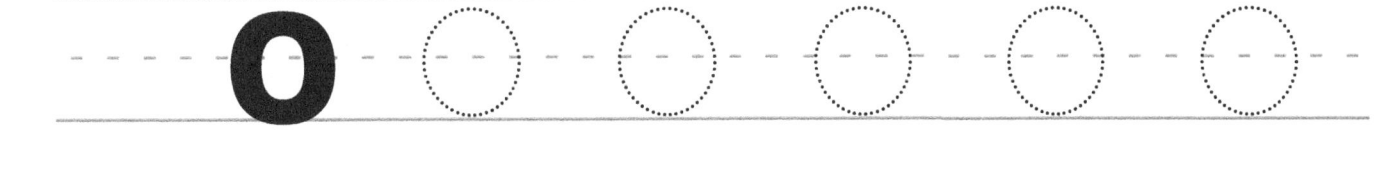

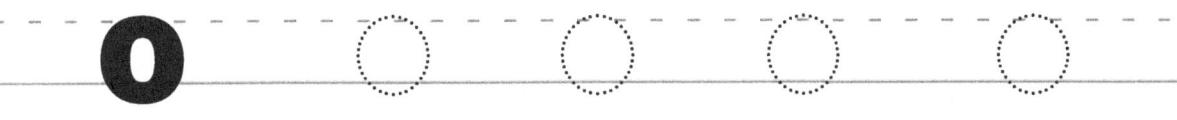

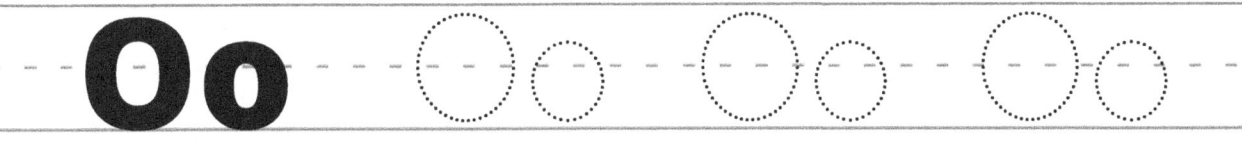

O O O O O O

o o o o o

Oo Oo Oo Oo

Orange Orange

P Pizza

P P P P P P

p p p p p p

Pp Pp Pp Pp

Place Place

Q Quality

Q Q Q Q Q Q

q q q q q q

Qq Qq Qq Qq

Quarter Quarter

R Rose

R R R R R R

r r r r r r

Rr Rr Rr Rr Rr

Radio Radio

S Soup

S S S S S S S

s s s s s s s s

Ss Ss Ss Ss   Ss

Salade Salade

T Taxi

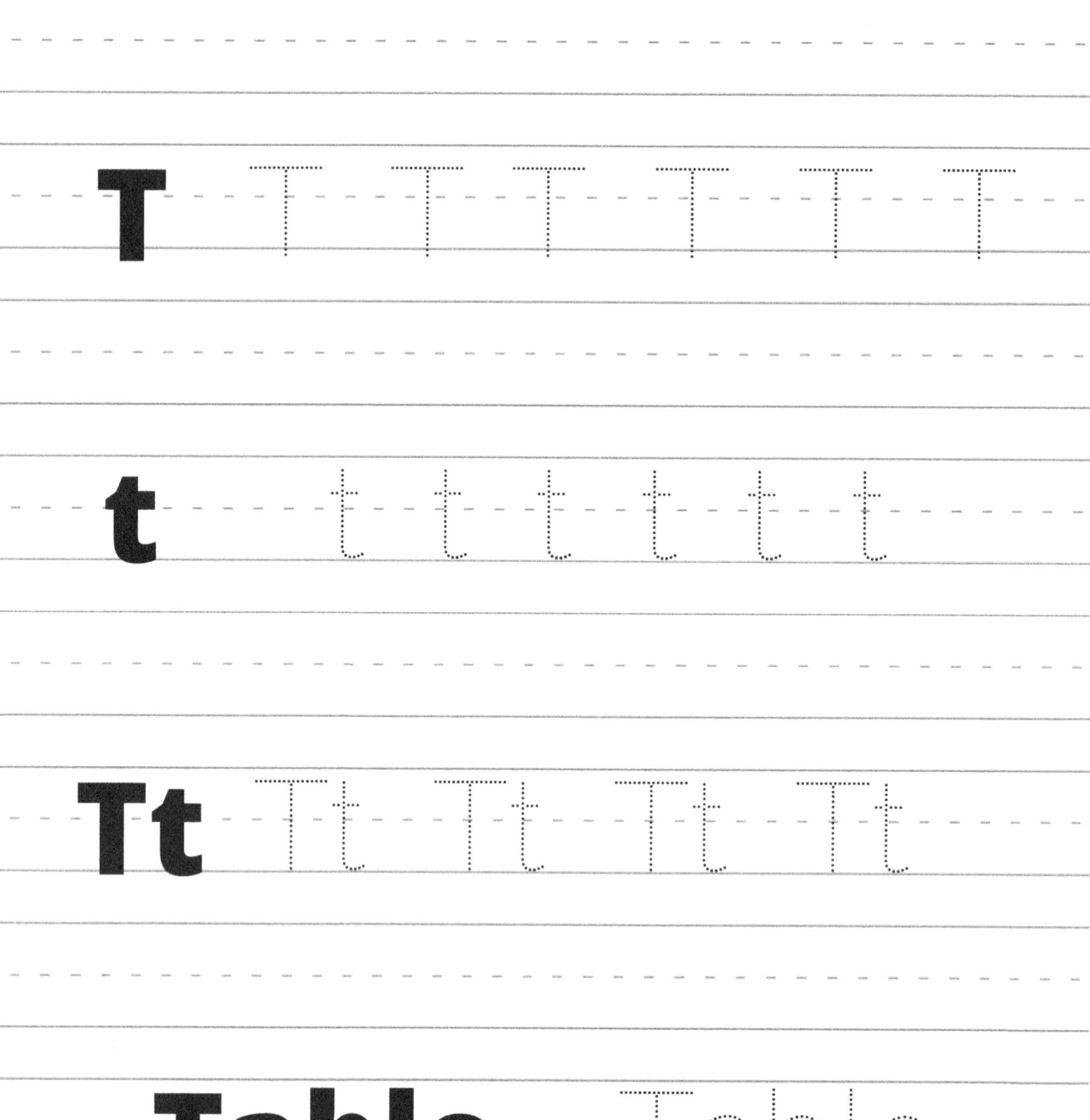

T T T T T T T T

t t t t t t t

Tt Tt Tt Tt Tt

Table Table

U   Unicorn

U   U U U U U

u   u u u u u u

Uu   Uu Uu Uu

Univers   Univers

V   Valley

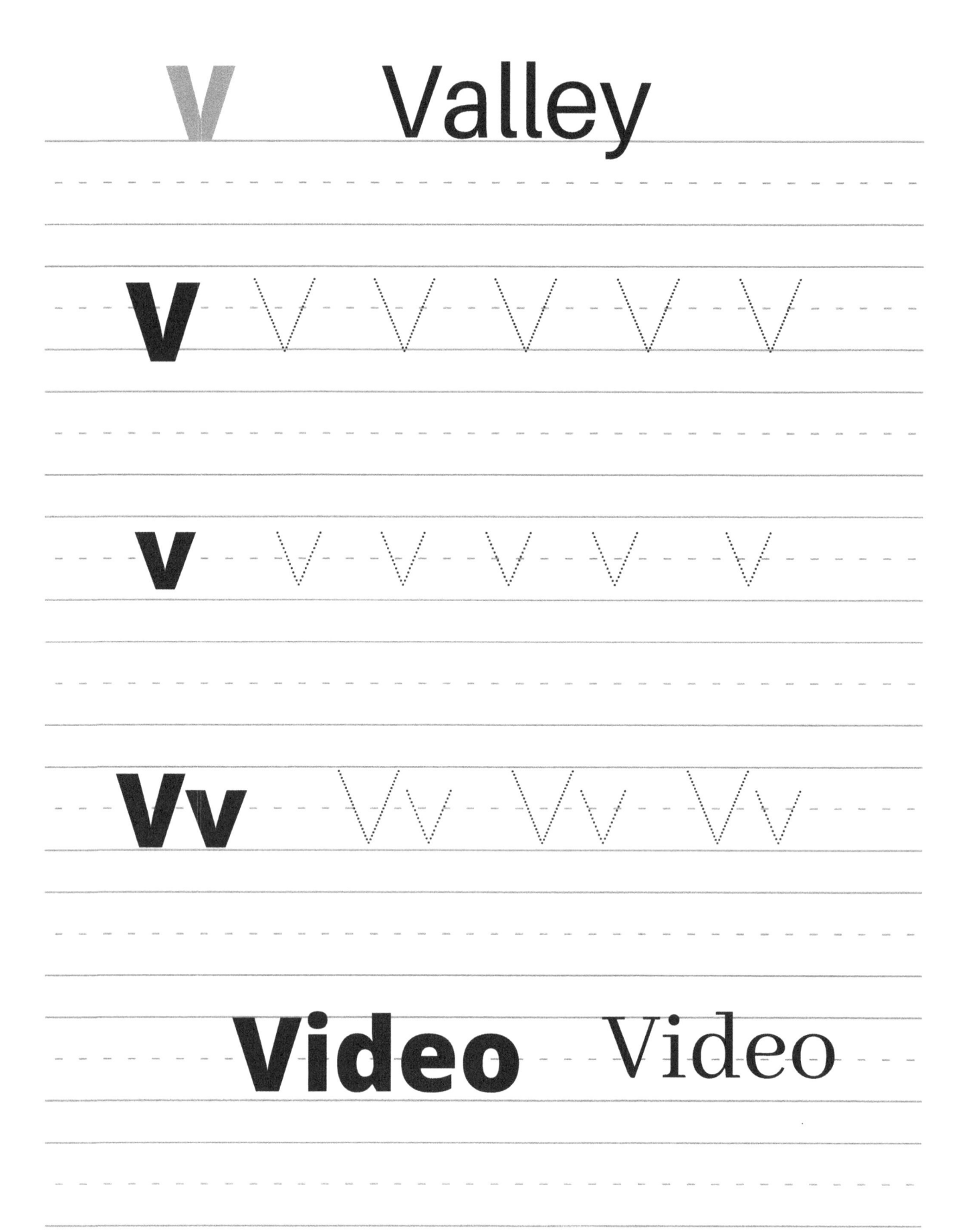

V   V V V V V

V   v v v v v

Vv   Vv Vv Vv Vv

Video   Video

W Wapiti

W W W W W

w w w w w

Ww Ww Ww

Web Web

X Xavier

X X X X X X

x x x x x

Xx Xx Xx Xx

Exercise
Exercise

Y Yacht

Y Y Y Y Y Y

y y y y y y y

Yy Yy Yy Yy Yy

Yoyo Yoyo

Z   Zèbra

Z Z Z Z Z Z

z z z z z z

Zz Zz Zz Zz Zz

Zoo Zoo

NUMBRES

1 1 1 1 1 1 1 1 1

One One One

One Pencil

One Pencil

2

2 2 2 2 2

Two Two Deux

Two Bananas

Two Bananas

3 Three

3 3 3 3 3 3

Three Three Three

Three books

Trois books

4 Four

4 4 4 4 4 4

Four Four

Four Nights

Four Nights

5   Five

5   5   5   5   5   5

Five   Five   Five

Five Nights

Five Nights

6 Six

6 6 6 6 6 6 6

Six Six Six Six

Six years

Six years

7 Seven

7 7 7 7 7 7 7

Seven

Seven Days

Seven Days

8 Eight

8 8 8 8 8 8

Eight Eight Eight

Eight Kids

Eight Kids

9 Nine

9 9 9 9 9 9

Nine Nine Nine

Nine Véhicules

Nine Véhicules

10 Ten

10 10 10 10 10

Ten Ten Ten

Ten Weeks

Ten Weeks

WORDS

Life Life

France France

Love Love

Face Face

Vacation Vacation

Girl Girl

Energy Energy

Boy Boy

Kind Kind

Escargot Escargot

Space Space

Earth Earth

Mouse Mouse

Celebrate Celebrate

Movie Movie

Lion Lion

Farine Farine

Art Art

Spirit Spirit

Good Good

Life Life

Smart Smart

Rabbit Rabbit

Gentle Gentle

Positive Positive

King King

Prince Prince

Palace Palace

Courage Courage

Création Great

Aspect Aspect

Papillon Papillon

Dream Dream

Passion Passion

Country Country

Lady Lady

Giraffe Giraffe

Women Women

Eraser Eraser

Smile Smile

Shop Shop

Novel Novel

Sky Sky

World World

Laugh Laugh

Beach Beach

Beauty Beauty

Brilliant Brilliant

Night Night

Café Café

Science Science

Chicken Chicken

Fish Fish

Head Head

Nose Nose

Hand Hand

Heart Heart

Foot Foot

Alaska Alaska

Ballet Ballet

Baguette

Baguette

Young Young

Married Married

Hôtel Hôtel

Novel Novel

Omelette
Omelette

Massage Massage

Galerie Galerie

Road Road

Plane Plane

Héritage Héritage

Jewerly Jewerly

Candy Candy

Honey Honey

Bread Bread

Pizza Pizza

Soirée Soirée

Nephew Nephew

Aunt Aunt

Europe Europe

Asia Asia

Eagle Eagle

Baleine Baleine

Toast Toast

Cat Cat

Horse
Horse

Strawberry Strawberry

Ice Cream

Ice Cream

Milk Milk

Fromage

Fromage

Pasta Pasta

Coffee Coffee

Watermelon

Watermelon

Orange Orange

Banana Banana

Sweet Sweet

Blueberry Blueberry

Citron Citron

Melon Melon

Sun   Sun

Planet Planet

Vénus   Vénus

Lune   Lune

Jupiter Jupiter

Saturne Saturne

Uranus Uranus

Neptune Neptune

Pluton
Pluton

Cartoon
Cartoon

Peace   Peace

Relationship
Relationship

Mile   Mile

Honeybee
Honeybee

Nöel Noel Noel

Happy Year
Happy Year

Fan Fan Fan

Fantastic
Fantastic

Cheese Cheese

Light Light

Burger Burger

Food Food

Prince Prince

Princess Princess

State State

Freedom Freedom

Hope Hope

COLOURS

White White

Black Black

Red Red

Green Green

Blue   Blue

Yellow   Yellow

Gris   Gris

Marron   Marron

Orange   Orange

Violet

Violet

Yellow orange

Yellow orange

Red Violet

Red Violet

Apricot

Apricot

SCHOOL SUPPLIES

School Box

School Box

Pencils

Pencils

Colouring Pencils

Colouring Pencils

Files

Files

Lunch Box

Lunch Box

Sharpie

Sharpie

highlighters

highlighters

Eraser

Eraser

sharpener

Sharpener

a ballpoint pen

a Ballpoint pen

Calculator

Calculator

Journal

Journal

Pencil Case

Pencil Case

Glue

Glue

Notebook

Notebook

Graph Paper

Graph Paper

PLANETS

Earth Earth

Mars Mars

Venus Venus

Jupiter Jupiter

Saturn Saturn

Mercury Mercury

Uranus Uranus

Neptune Neptune

SENTENCES

Welcome Home

Welcome Home

I Love My Family

I Love My Family

I Read To Learn

I Read To Learn

I Like Puppies

I Like Puppies

Respect is The Best

Respect is The Best

Mothers are Strong

Mothers are Strong

I'm Full of Energy

I'm Full of Energy

Jack Reads a Book

Jack Reads a Book

Our House is Clean

Our House is Clean

The Baby is Walking

The Baby is Walking

Noël is Coming

Noël is Coming

Do you Like Sports?

Do you Like Sports?

Can I borrow your Basket?

Can I borrow your Basket?

Can I Teach you?

Can I Teach you?

COUNTRIES

Albania Albania

America America

Australia Australia

Austria Austria

Brazil Brazil

Bahamas Bahamas

Belgium Belgium

Belarus Belarus

Bahrain Bahrain

Colombia Colombia

Canada Canada

Chile Chile

China China

Cambodia Cambodia

Denmark

Djibouti

Dominica

Egypt Egypt

Equador Equador

Estonia Estonia

Ethiopia

Ethiopia

France France

Finland Finland

Germany Germany

Georgia Georgia

Greece Greece

Hungary   Hungary

India   India

Italy   Italy

Iceland   Iceland

Japan   Japan

Jordan Jordan

Korea Korea

Kosovo Kosovo

Luxembourg

Luxembourg

Malaysia Malaysia

Norway Norway

Portugal Portugal

Qatar Qatar

Russia Russia

Romania Romania

Singapore
Singapore

Sweden Sweden

Spain Spain

Turkey Turkey

Uruguay Uruguay

Zambia Zambia

United Kingdom

United Kingdom

DRAWING

Apple   Apple

Bus Bus

Dinosaur

Dinosaur

Cow Cow

Lion Lion

Sheep Sheep

Fish Fish

Sun Sun

Dolphin Dolphin

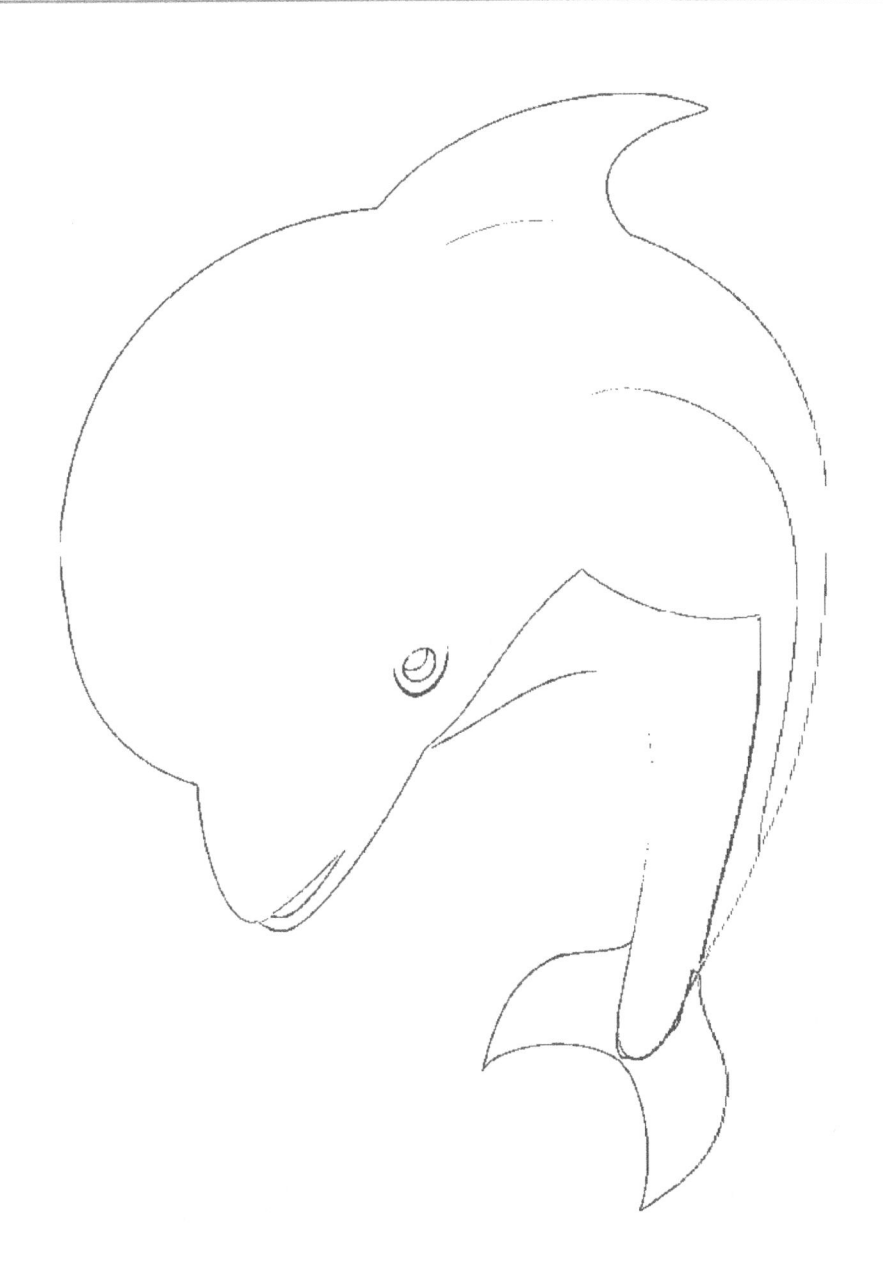

BRAVO CHAMPION

Made in United States
Orlando, FL
30 November 2023